LINCOLN CHRISTIAN COLL
P9-CQB-623

What They're Saying about This Guide

"Judy Comstock provides timely information and creative approaches and cutting-edge ideas for some of the greatest leadership needs in children's ministry. This book is a refreshing and a much needed guide to the veteran as well as the novice children's leader on the essentials of establishing and developing a children's ministry with excellence."
—**M. Kurt Jarvis**, Disciple Making Ministries Director, INCM Board of Directors, The Christian and Missionary Alliance Metropolitan District

"Judy Comstock's love for kids and those who minister to them is second to none. She's produced a 'home run' with this practical help for church leaders."
—**Jim Wideman**, author, leadership coach, children's ministry consultant

"This ministry guide lays out many basics of children's ministry. Judy Comstock uses the experiences from her church staff, along with input from other churches, to bring us suggestions. Her emphasis on first impressions hits the mark. Comstock brings to our attention the various opportunities for ministry with children, besides the obvious one of teaching. She reminds us that everyone does not have the gift of teaching and how important it is to find the gifts that God has given volunteers and connect them with specific opportunities for ministry. Children's ministry today must work in tandem with other ministries in the church. As Comstock suggests, this is the attribute of a healthy children's ministry."
—**Delia Halverson**, Faith Discovery Ministries

Abingdon Press & The Church of the Resurrection
Ministry Guides

Children's Ministry

Judy Comstock
Adam Hamilton, Series Editor

ABINGDON PRESS
Nashville

CHILDREN'S MINISTRY

Copyright © 2006 by Abingdon Press

All rights reserved.

No part of this work may be reproduced or transmitted in any form or by any means, electronic or mechanical, including photocopying and recording, or by any information storage or retrieval system, except as may be expressly permitted by the 1976 Copyright Act or in writing from the publisher. Requests for permission can be addressed to Abingdon Press, P.O. Box 801, 201 Eighth Avenue South, Nashville, TN 37202-0801, or e-mailed to permissions@abingdonpress.com.

This book is printed on acid-free paper.

Library of Congress Cataloging-in-Publication Data

Comstock, Judy, 1950-
Children's Ministry : The Church of the Resurrection / Judy Comstock.
p. cm. — (Ministry guides 1)
ISBN 0-687-33413-6 (binding: pbk., adhesive : alk. paper)
1. Church work with children—Handbooks, manuals, etc. I. Title. II. Series.

BV639.C4C645 2006
259'.22—dc22

2006005002

Scripture taken from the HOLY BIBLE, NEW INTERNATIONAL VERSION®. Copyright © 1973, 1978, 1984 by International Bible Society. Used by permission of Zondervan Publishing House. All rights reserved.

06 07 08 09 10 11 12 13 14 15—10 9 8 7 6 5 4 3 2 1
MANUFACTURED IN THE UNITED STATES OF AMERICA

115980

Foreword

Children are often the entry point for families in joining a church—churches that recognize this are on their way to vitality and growth. But, it's also a fact that children are one of the most demanding audiences in the church. This audience comes in all sizes, colors, shapes, and personalities. As unpredictable as they can be, these children must be kept safe, but given freedom. They have to be entertained, but taught well. Wiggling or still, crying or laughing, loud or quiet, they need to be loved in a big way.

That's where the Abingdon Press & The Church of the Resurrection *Children's Ministry* guide comes in. With energy and an enthusiastic can-do attitude, Judy Comstock gives practical how-to information for laypeople—and professionals—involved in this special ministry. She has developed ways to bring children in, ways to bring in their families, and ways to bring in their friends. It's good, practical advice that will help children's workers be off and running.

At The Church of the Resurrection, we live daily with the goal to help people become deeply committed Christians. More than nominally religious. More than the Sunday pew holder. More than the spectator. We know these same people become more by doing more. We begin with the knowledge that people want the church to be theirs. They want to know God has a place for them. With that in mind, we recognized from the very start that specialized ministries utilizing the skills and talents of laypeople are fundamental to church life.

A church on the move will have specialized ministries capitalizing on the skills and talents of laypeople. They are your keys to succeed.

In developing these guides, we listened to the requests of smaller churches for practical resources to enlist laypeople for this purpose. These economical guides, written by proven leaders at our church, will serve as essential resources for innovative, creative, and, more than likely, nontraditional church workers who have little or no budget to work with. With these guides in hand, your laypeople will be ready to plunge into the work with excitement and courage instead of tentatively approaching it on tiptoe.

At the core of these guides is the belief that anything is possible. It's a challenge, but it's a truth. God can and does use us all—with that conviction we bring hope to the world.

Adam Hamilton
Senior Pastor
The Church of the Resurrection
Leawood, Kansas

CHAPTER ONE

Making Children's Ministry the Flagship

Each summer a sailing adventure called the Tall Ships Challenge alternates between the Atlantic, the Great Lakes, and the Pacific coasts of North America. On each ship, volunteers sign up with experienced paid crew members to form a remarkable team. This impressive race draws thousands of spectators. The shape of the ships, the rigging, and the wooden details are notable on these grand sailing vessels. Even more notable is the significant impact the tall ships had on history.

Churches that raise the value of Children's Ministry are making an impact, as well. Even adults with no direct connection as parents or volunteers recognize the importance of our work and routinely bring their friends through the children's area to describe the exciting things that are happening. Sadly, the churches who do not consider younger members of the family will crash into the rocks. Statistician George Barna, author of *Transforming Children into Spiritual Champions* (Regal Books, 2003), confirms the importance of the work done by Children's Ministry leaders. Barna's message rings clear that the emerging generation is impacting the emerging church.

Growing up in a culture with few absolutes has not eliminated opinions and interests in spiritual things for today's children. The economic sway they have is described in James McNeal's book *Kids as Customers* (Lexington Books, 1992). In the article "How well marketing works on kids, what the numbers say" (*Curriculum Review*, no. 42, September 2002), McNeal discusses the fact that children ages two to fourteen directly influence over $188 billion in spending. Kristen Harmeling, a marketing expert on the consumer habits of children, reports that "Before, kids had a say in food; now, they have a say in everything." They have a voice in everything from selecting the family car to deciding the site for the family vacation, she says (Yankelovich Youth Monitor, "Taking Marketing Productivity Higher," 2005).

By assessing our programs and facilities through the eyes of a family with children, we can determine our strengths and discover where adjustments are needed. A family's first impression of Children's Ministries may be the deciding factor for repeat visits. Does the atmosphere indicate that kids count? Providing a safe, clean setting is important to parents. Kids value relationships and the fun factor.

First Impressions . . . All Hands on Deck

Starting at the front door of the church building, let's take an imaginary tour through the eyes of that visiting family.

As we step inside, who will answer their questions about the children's classroom locations? The programs?

- **Post** greeters at every entrance. These "first friendly faces" should acknowledge the children and direct or escort the family to the children's area.
- **Recruit** a Children's Ministry Hospitality Team. The welcoming team members will be ready to answer

questions about Children's Ministry. Staffing a Children's Information Booth can connect families to your ministry.

Where are the nursery and Sunday school classrooms? As with real estate, location is important. Assess your floor plans through the eyes of parents with young children. In doing so, one church decided to rearrange the room assignments to move the nursery nearer the sanctuary. The benefit of this change was noted.

How will I be contacted if my child needs me? Ask parents to leave their cell phone number on the class roster. Encourage parents to set their cell phones on vibrate. Cell phones provide a simple paging solution. Another method is an usher card on which the parents provide their names. The usher will note their pew location and some identifiable indicator, such as the color of the dad's shirt. The usher can use the card to locate the parent in case of an emergency.

How do I enroll my child? Provide a registration form requesting the child's name, birthdate, address, phone number, a description of the child's unique needs, and parental information. A computer savvy volunteer can add a Children's Ministry page to your church's website. Information on programs and upcoming events may be routinely posted. Keeping the information current is important. Consider adding the convenient option of preregistering children for events and programs on the website. Whether visitor information is noted in your church's computer database or a card file, keeping a record on prospects and members for follow-up and future contact is wise.

What measures are taken so my child is not released to the wrong person? A claim-check approach is an effective security measure. At check-in, the parent is given a numbered tag and the matching numbered tag is pinned to the child's clothing. Laminate the colored card stock tags to extend the use. Parents present the tag at the close of the class time when calling for their child. (See further discussion on page 29.)

How will you know about my child's allergy? Encourage parents to record their child's unique needs on the registration form. Ask them to place a colored sticker dot on the child's nametag or "claim-check" tag to alert the teachers. Colored wristbands made from *tyvek®* can serve the same purpose. Parents should indicate their child's specific need or allergy on the band, then place it on their child's wrist. A "lifetime supply" (five hundred wristbands) can be purchased for about $20 through suppliers such as www.wristbandexpress.com.

Housekeeping . . . Swab the Decks

Children's Ministry requires a lot of stuff (supplies), and working with children can be messy. Even so, parents expect clean facilities, especially when their children are young.

As you walk into the children's area, are there distinct odors?

- **Place** soiled diapers in plastic bags. Use recycled shopping or grocery produce bags. Tie the bag and discard it in a covered plastic-lined container. Wipe the changing area with disinfectant. One part bleach to three parts water is a safe, economical solution.

- **Disinfect** toys. Cleaning toys in the top shelf of a dishwasher or regularly wiping them with a bleach-water solution will kill germs and eliminate unpleasant odors.

Does the play area in the early childhood classrooms have an appropriate number of toys? Are the shelves overstocked? Are there enough toys?

- **Reserve** the right to discard donated toys. While donations are appreciated, the church often becomes the benefactor of old, broken items. Be selective about what you keep.
- **Schedule** a department gift shower. List specific items that are needed or register at a store in your community, such as Babies "R" Us or a large discount retailer. Decorate for the party. Serve cookies and punch to the guests. Invite a few key volunteers to open the gifts. This fun approach to stocking cabinets may become an annual event.
- **Avoid** the temptation to overstock the classrooms. Even if your church provides a generous budget for Children's Ministries, it's best to not have an overabundance of toys in the classroom. Rotate the toys by storing unused items in cabinets or plastic tubs. This approach can add anticipation and build some surprises into each week. Reinforce the theme for the week by displaying toys that connect easily to the lesson.

Décor . . . Attention!

On our imaginary walk, what do you see on the walls in the children's area? Is there evidence that kids are welcome here? Artist Bruce Barry (www.wackyworld.com) has created some fantastic presentations. However, most of us cannot afford his impressive three-dimensional, interactive themes.

What are some affordable decorating methods?

- **Photograph** and enlarge pictures of children. Hang photos enlarged to at least eighteen-inch square and matted on foam core. Processing in black and white adds an artistic flair. Obtain written permission from parents before taking a child's picture.
- **Do-it-yourself.** Check out Randy Triplett's website gallery of creative Children's Ministry designs (www.painteroffun.com). With the help of a few volunteers, an entire room can be created in a few hours using his Theme Room Decorating Kits. Or, make transparency patterns from copyright-free coloring books. Let your imagination soar.

At Church of the Resurrection, the hallways depict outdoor scenes common to Kansas City. Scriptures are lettered on each wall. Since being a light to the world is a focus for the church, various forms of light are also incorporated. A candle in a window, a porch light, rays of sunlight, a rainbow, a lantern, and fireflies help make the connection. When asked why the walls are painted like this, a second grader answered, "It's so when I'm driving around and see a place, it will make me think of my church." She got it! What do you want your walls to say?

What can we do with a leased building?

A decorating challenge exists for churches leasing a facility such as a school.

- **Signage** is needed outside the building for directions to the site, but inside the building, signs help create an atmosphere. Colorful placards with pictures of happy children may be hung on Sunday morning from the grid bars of dropped ceilings. Portable fencing or large carpet remnants can create designated play areas. Portable Church Industries provides a "soup-to-nuts" approach for the church on the move.

- **Affordable** canvas. One decorating solution that works in leased space is to airbrush enlarged ministry logos and scenes on economical bed sheets. The cloth can be hung on a wall to add color and connection.

The Fun Factor

Children can learn in an "un-fun" place. However, if given a choice to attend, most children will weigh their decision with an enjoyment appraisal. Parents want their child to increase in knowledge, but their most common question to the child at the close of the programming hour is, "Did you have fun?"

- **Establish** an appropriate ratio of adults to children. To facilitate positive relationships with leaders and other kids, consider a 1:7 adult-to-child ratio for the preschool age levels and 1:10 for the elementary grades. (Keep in mind the two-person rule discussed on page 28.)
- **Engage** the children. Waiting for the first activity at the start of the class time is boring. Some children create their own activity that may result in inappropriate behavior. From the moment the first child enters the classroom, have interactive options ready to go.

Floor games

Four Square is a popular playground game. Use a roll of electrical tape to create the game grid on the classroom floor. A nerf-type playground ball can be used with this fun game. Consider the size of your classrooms if using this active game.

Plastic shoe box activity centers

Play dough, sticky wicks, and other craft tools can be stored and rotated in a variety of activity centers. Curriculum publishers routinely include ideas that connect the story or mission project to the lesson theme.

Leading the Way

On our imaginary walk, did you note places where change is needed? Improving the first impression, taking care of housekeeping needs, and adding kid-friendly decorating techniques are important. Even more important is the link to spiritual exploration.

Last fall, one of our fifth graders invited a friend to join him on Wednesday nights at a program designed for their grade level. Before long, the friend started coming to Sunday school. This new boy, who had no background in religious education, was soon telling his parents that he wanted them to be a "church family." Dynamic spiritual changes occurred as Children's Ministry reached into their home. Only months later, members of this family were baptized and joined the church. Children's Ministry is helping the church grow numerically and spiritually.

CHAPTER TWO

Recruiting Volunteers . . . the Right Bait

Why would a woman dress in white, wrap a yellow feather boa around her neck, tie an orange beak over her nose, and "cluck" an entire melodrama in front of her family and friends? Staff members from a Michigan public school system performed in a citywide variety show in which participation was not mandatory, so why did seventy adults get involved? The answers are simple. We were asked to participate. We used our talents. Yes, talent! The purpose was important. The money we raised put computers in the classrooms. It felt good to be part of something important. And, we had fun!

Adults are often offered the opportunity to volunteer for organizations that impact children. Our ministry volunteer needs can get lost in society's requests unless the mission is articulated, expectations defined, and the benefits celebrated.

Fishing Buddies

Calculating specific volunteer needs and setting realistic job expectations is an important first step.

- **Divide** traditional jobs into smaller tasks. Finding one person willing to fulfill all of the duties of certain positions can be difficult. Some jobs are not in the classroom, but support the classroom teacher.

  An important pre-class task is preparing the lesson teaching aids and crafts for the lesson. Invite an organized volunteer to work behind the scenes to prepare consumable items needed in each classroom. On Sunday, when the guides (teachers) arrive, the supply bin is ready for them. If the lesson calls for ribbons, the volunteer has counted, cut, and prepared them. Instead of thinking about glue sticks, the teachers can concentrate on the story, the Bible theme activities, and the needs of individual children.
- **Strive** for diverse teams. Connect experienced volunteers with novices. Recruit for a gender mix. Children need to connect with women and men who appreciate the faith journey. Sunday school has traditionally been a place for mothers, but dads enjoy time with their children too.
- **Clearly** define expectations. Provide realistic written job descriptions for your dream team. Determine the tenure and the number of times each month the volunteer is expected to participate. Consistency will help the children establish trusting relationships with the leaders.

One church made a radical decision to suspend Sunday school on four holiday weekends. Families worship together in the sanctuary on Easter, Memorial Day weekend, Labor Day weekend, and Christmas. Youth and adult Sunday school classes are also suspended, but a nursery is provided. Volunteers appreciate this accommodation.

Who Is in the Boat?

Volunteers want to use their skills or know that training is provided. Adult and youth volunteers like connecting in a friendly, fulfilling atmosphere. Recruiting for the buddy system may include these areas:

Classroom assignments

- **Age/Grade Coordinators:** lead quarterly team meetings, guide class time.
- **Guides:** teach, assist at check-in/checkout, lead small group discussions.
- **Parent/Youth Helpers:** assist with room set-up, crafts, snacks, and cleanup.

Administrative assignments

- **Prayer Team:** meets weekly and for special needs.
- **Writers:** use curriculum and resources so lesson plans meet your church needs.
- **Crafters and Bulletin Board Artists:** plan/implement weekly and seasonal ideas.
- **Supply Prep Team:** gathers and sorts classroom teaching supplies.
- **Hospitality Team:** takes care of data entry and greets members and visitors.
- **Library Team:** purchases, stocks, organizes books and videos.
- **Mission Committee:** selects projects and promotes participation.
- **Special Event Teams:** operate specific to events.
- **Leadership Board Members:** support Children's Ministry and organize related events.

Large group assignments

- **Musicians:** vocal and instrumental.
- **Storytellers/Actors/Puppeteers.**
- **Tech/Sound Support:** runs equipment for music or videos that enhance the presentations. Youth volunteers enjoy this assignment.

Baiting the Hook

My father-in-law's skills as a fisherman included his ability to craft elaborate lures using hooks disguised as colorful feathers, plastic insects, and slimy worms. Some anglers think the color of the bait impacts success. Others say the wrist actions determine the catch. Even the time of day is a consideration. People who fish agree that nothing is caught unless the bait is offered.

What approaches will help us get the volunteers we need?

Recruiting volunteers in Children's Ministries should include an invitation that is both positive and strategic.

- **Kids** invite their moms and dads. Use an "I Choose You" sticker. Children who want their parents to help in the classroom will present their mom or dad with a sticker. If the kids like the program, their parents will hear about it.
- **Register** children of volunteers early. This approach is effective for midweek and special events, such as Vacation Bible Camp. Allow early registration for the children of volunteers. At a later date a general registration will fill the remaining spots on the class rosters. This works for popular programs!

OOPS

Here is a cute idea we tried, and then tried again. Persistence did not improve the results. In the spring, a beautiful rolled-frosting sheet cake topped with a model of our logo was displayed in the narthex. An announcement and banner promoted the idea that volunteering for the summer in Children's Ministry is "a piece of cake." Everyone who signed up was given a slice. We got a few volunteers, but not the number we sought. Here is the lesson we learned: cake is not what prompts a volunteer commitment.

- **Current** volunteers invite a friend. Adults who do not have young children may hear volunteers talk about their positive experiences in the ministry. Designate a "Shadow Sunday." Encourage volunteers to invite a friend to join them in the classroom to observe the meaningful interactions and see how volunteering works.
- **Phone** blitz. Church members not currently serving in any area are called. Describe the opportunities and invite those members to get involved. You may have some success, but this cannot be your primary approach.
- **Involve** the kids. "You'll have it made in the shade" is a fun theme. Children wearing giant sunglasses join their parent(s) and the greeters posted at the entrance to the church. As church members arrive for the worship service, they smile at the sight of the kids and are offered a flier describing volunteer opportunities in Children's Ministries.

- **Invite** a team of volunteers to promote. Parents may start volunteering when their children are young. As they move up with the class, solid and enduring relationships are built. This popular approach works!

How to Cast the Line

Most volunteers are not professional educators. Frequently they are moms and dads working in a range of careers. Using curriculum and lesson plans is not part of many volunteers' daily routine. Managing other people's kids is awkward for most adults. Then there are the theological issues, such as teaching children to pray, leading a child to Christ, and knowing Bible answers.

How can we train our volunteers?

A survey could provide insight into your volunteers' greatest needs. Ask them what skills they want to improve.

- **Consider** quarterly teacher-training sessions. Start the Sunday school year focusing on child safety procedures and the program schedule. Limit the meeting length from one to two hours. Describe how you will keep them informed. Distribute the curriculum at the meeting and review the use.
- **Provide** training on specific topics. Invite an expert on issues such as discipline to be the guest speaker. Schoolteachers have great ideas on preventive discipline, responsive discipline, and other teaching strategies. Ask the guest trainer if you may videotape the presentation for volunteers to review.
- **Teaching** library. Catalog audio and video tapes, books, magazines, and downloadable articles. Volunteers may borrow from this library. Their confidence will be boosted and skills improved as you provide information on topics such as teaching a child how to pray, leading a child to Christ, and guiding a small group discussion. *Teach Kids!* from Child Evangelism Fellowship, Group Publishing's *Children's Ministry Magazine,* and *Children's Teacher* from Cokesbury are periodicals that regularly

include effective teaching strategies. Downloadable material is available at sites such as www.christianity today.com and www.christiancrafters.com.

- **Regional** seminars. Curriculum publishers, the International Network of Children's Ministries, and denominational offices offer seminars, usually on Saturdays. Volunteers will leave with improved skills and renewed passion for reaching and teaching children.

Fish Tales!

Children's Ministries is a great place to volunteer. Celebrate successes. Help volunteers enjoy the experience. A positive perspective makes recruiting easier. Word gets around about the ministry. Make it the flagship . . . not a sinking ship!

How can we present the benefits of volunteering?

- **Tell** the story. Use the church newsletter, videos, posters, and displays to describe the effect of Children's Ministry.
- **Make** your volunteers visible. Create volunteer name badges. Lanyards may identify their screened and approved status. Brightly colored lanyards also promote the idea of being on "the team." If someone asks what the yellow lanyards signify, tell them how to connect as a volunteer.
- **Advertise** with trinkets. Imprint your ministry logo and name on gadgets like license plate frames and pens. With the theme "Building His Kingdom, Reaching His Kids," we gave away pocket-size tape measures. A crafter's economical sticker

machine can be used to personalize trinkets and advertise the ministry.

How can we make volunteers feel special?

- **Super** Soda Sunday. Invite teachers to visit the soda bar in a classroom or the hall. Selecting cherry or vanilla flavor for their soft drink is fun. Add colorful straws to get smiles and surprisingly positive responses.
- **Sweet** Sunday. Attach a piece of miniature candy to an inspirational poem and distribute your message of gratitude to your teachers. They will love the surprise and appreciate the thanks.
- **Family** Skating Party. Parents and children place donations in skate shoes outside each classroom for "take your teacher skating" night. Everyone is invited, but teachers and their families are the special guests.
- **Communication.** Personal notes serve to reinforce the worth of volunteers. Celebrate and mourn life events. Pray for and with volunteers. Keep your volunteers informed through a weekly e-mail, phone call, or face-to-face time. Listen to their perspective. Respect their opinions. In other words, build a team!

A pastor I know of says that one of the "hardest hoops to hop through" is getting the Children's Ministry director to move from a doer role to one of leading and equipping. That is a huge part of recruiting volunteers. When your responsibilities seem overwhelming, pray Luke 10:2 that the Lord will send the help you need. Extending training opportunities to the volunteers goes hand-in-hand with the invitation to get involved. Then, release them to do their job that multiplies your efforts. Some people are not suited for Children's Ministry. Accept their decline. Some individuals will say yes! Help them find great fulfillment. Never give up! The rewards and joys are eternal.

CHAPTER THREE

Screening, Security, and Safety . . . Life Jackets

One summer I visited Branson, a family friendly site nestled in the beautiful hills of southern Missouri. My husband and I rode on a tourist attraction called The Duck. From this amphibious vehicle we saw spectacular sites around the city. Interesting facts were described as we quacked, literally, at the passengers riding in other Ducks. When we neared Table Rock Lake, the captain stopped to illustrate the safety features we should know. He taught us how to put on a life jacket and described important precautions we might use in the water.

As Captain of the *USS Children's Ministries*, we, too, must calculate measures that will keep everyone in our care from harm's way. Step one is to determine the suitability of individuals who work with the children. Next, we should create a secure environment. Procedures for emergency conditions also need to be clearly defined. Even then, we cannot just float. Vigilantly maintaining a safe setting requires a constant watchful eye.

Screening

Our work is serious business. To safeguard the physical and emotional welfare of the children requires proactive measures. The policies your church implements should apply to paid staff and volunteers. According to attorney J. David Epstein, in *How to Protect Your Children's Ministry from Liability* (Gospel Light Publishing, 1995), the courts put volunteers in the same category as employees.

How can we reduce the risk of allowing unsafe people, particularly sexual predators, to be with the children?

- **Screen** all staff members and volunteers. Gather information on an "Application to Work with Minors." The National Database provides a broad search of 250 million records from the 3,600 counties that report sexual crimes. This search includes the National Sexual Offender list and a Social Security trace. Background search services are available for a fee through organizations such as www.churchstaffing.com and Church Volunteer Central. Your denominational headquarters and church's insurance company may also provide a screening service. In some communities the local police department may assist in the screening process. Several states make it difficult to obtain information on sexual offenders. Most states close the records of juvenile offenders. Even so, churches large and small are held accountable to determine the safety of volunteers who work with minors.
- **Require** at least two unrelated references. Document comments made by the references you

contact. Their responses can be by mail or telephone. The pastor's insight on an applicant's suitability is valuable. Some churches require six to twelve months of regular attendance or membership to qualify as a volunteer. Contact the applicant's previous church to learn more on his or her character.

- **Keep** all screening results confidential. Indicate on the form that signing the document grants permission for the church to contact references and to perform an investigation, which includes contacting law enforcement agencies. The clergy and department director may review the application to validate the information. Applicants who have passed the initial screening should be interviewed before final approval.

- **Reject** any applicant with questionable suitability. If questions are raised about the candidate, the screener should notify the department director. Wording on your policy might be, *"Persons alleged and convicted of sexual abuse, past or present, will not be considered as volunteers for minors."* Sexual misconduct is not the only disqualifying criterion. Emotional instability and abusive history also disqualify an individual who would have direct contact with a minor.

A Child Protection Policy and an application form are available on the volunteer section of the www.kidscor.org website.

Supervising

Approved volunteers should wear an identifiable nametag. They may be asked to wear the same color lanyard or shirt. Posting photographs of approved volunteers outside the classrooms is beneficial. This strategy enhances community as parents connect names and faces. It is also a safety precaution.

What approaches help in maintaining a secure environment?

- **Mandate** the two-person rule. At least two nonrelated persons must be present before a child can be checked into the classroom.
- **Make** unannounced visits to classrooms. Let volunteers know that supervisors will randomly check their classroom whenever minors are present. A window in or near the door of the room makes it easier to observe classroom activities. Note blind spots in the room. Vigilance is necessary.
- **Report** all observed or suspected abusive incidents. The pastor or department director should investigate and document any reported incidents. If the media learns of an investigation, communication should come from the pastor's office or his or her designee. Do not deny, minimize, or blame. However, privacy and confidentiality must be guarded.

Occasionally a one-on-one meeting with a minor is needed. The meeting should take place in a well-lit, visible, public area. A staff member and/or the child's parents should be informed of the meeting.

Security

The exposure to liability increases during the classroom checkout. No matter the size of the church, issues related to child custody battles can heighten the danger.

How can we diminish the potential of releasing a child to the wrong person?

- **Alphabetical** or numbered check-in list. Attach a coded or numbered key tag or die-cut shape to the child's clothing. Provide the parents with a matching tag to present when calling for their child at the close of the class time. Some churches choose to use a numbered two-part adhesive label system, such as those available from www.churchnursery.com.

- **Computerized** check-in systems. Programs such as Shelby Check-In incorporate a barcode scan for each child. Scanning the barcode on a barcode reader at a computer station prompts a printer in the classroom that creates multiple copies of adhesive receipts for the parent, child, and attendance notebook. At the close of the session, the parent's receipt is presented and matched with the child's. A video clip of this system can be viewed on the www.kidscor.org website.

No matter the system, questions may arise regarding eleasing a child. If so, ask the adult calling for the child to rovide additional proof of identification. Have the information confirmed with the child's registration records. hotographs of the persons allowed to call for the child may e attached to the registration records. Ask for assistance rom a department supervisor or staff member. Sadly, feloious attempts to claim children can occur. Training our volnteers to be alert to questionable situations may help us void a crisis. Safety trumps familiarity every time.

Safe Physical Contact

Kids today are savvy, but their size and experiences still make them vulnerable to abuse. Boundaries are necessary, especially when physical contact is considered. Adults should recognize that by complying with safe-touch guidelines, they are better protected against false accusations.

Appropriate touch:

- Gently touch the child's shoulders, hands, arms, head and back to comfort, encourage, or redirect the child. Use high-fives and handshakes to celebrate.
- Sitting a crying preschooler on your lap to comfort the child is acceptable.

Inappropriate touch:

- Sitting older children on your lap.
- Kissing, demanding hugs, touching areas that would be covered by a swimsuit.
- Any touching to express power or for the pleasure or satisfaction of the caregiver.

Restroom Procedures and Guidelines

It is best if parents take their children to the restroom before bringing them to the classroom. If a child needs to use the restroom, consider these guidelines:

- **Two** unrelated adults escort the entire group of children for a restroom break.
- **Assign** a restroom supervisor for all classes. This person will verify that the restroom is clear of adults and youth. When the child enters the restroom, the supervisor should stay in a visible area outside the room. If the child is delayed longer than seems necessary, the supervisor should call the child's name to determine any problem.
- **If** preschool-age children request assistance, the adult volunteer may assist at the open door, never entering the stall with the child.
- **Ask** the parents of a special needs child to define their child's needs. At no time should the dignity of any child be compromised.
- **Diapering** procedures include universal precautions, such as wearing disposable gloves. Some

churches now call for the parents when a young child needs a diaper change.

- **Call** for parents to assist their child if he or she has an accident. Stock extra clothing for boys and girls in several preschool sizes.

Safe Sanctuaries: Reducing the Risk of Child Abuse in the Church by Joy Melton (Discipleship Resources, 1998) contains valuable information for churches when screening, security, and safety are considered.

Safety Emergency Plans

Take the attendance notebook with you when leading all of the children from the classroom. It can be used to confirm each child's presence. Also, display the class name on the notebook to use it as a sign. For emergencies, take a supply bag or backpack containing bottled water, adhesive bandages, a flashlight, tissues, a pen, and a whistle.

- **Fire Safety**. If smoke or fire is evident, the alarms should be activated and 911 called. Immediately account for all children and lead them quickly, but cautiously, to the exit designated on the posted evacuation map in your room. All children and leaders should meet at least fifty feet from the building at a predetermined location. Your local fire marshal can provide specific guidelines.
- **Storm Safety.** Severe weather may necessitate movement to an area of the building that is protected from high winds or flooding. Account for each child and escort them as a group to the safe space indicated on the posted evacuation map. Rather than dismissing the children to their parents, invite the parents to stay in the safe place with you until an "all clear" is given.

While an earthquake is not caused by weather, safety measures are appropriate. Move the children away from glass or shelves. A safe place to stand is in an inner doorway. Or, seek shelter under a sturdy table or against an interior wall away from bookcases or tall windows.

- **Physical Threat.** If violent danger is imminent or physically threatening conditions occur, call 911 immediately. Use a two-way radio, telephone, or intercom to inform the Ministry Department director of the danger. If escape from the building is not possible, police officers suggest creating an atmosphere that implies "no one is home." Calmly move the children away from the windows and doors. Turn off the lights. Stay silent. Volunteers should stay with the children until law enforcement officers give an "all clear" notice.

It is sad that emergency procedures might need to be implemented. Even sadder would be the panic that might follow if you were not prepared. I hope the plans uniquely specific to your church will be carefully considered and the responses will help you maintain an environment focused on safety.

CHAPTER FOUR

Connecting with Kids ... Reelin' Them In

My son reeled in his first fish at a Saturday morning fishing derby. The little lake near our home had been stocked with fish, and he was excited about catching a big one. A call from my husband's office suddenly changed our plans. So at the breakfast table, I was taught how to tie a hook on a line. Pull the end of the line through the hook and wrap the end several times around the line above the hook. Then, tuck the end inside the wound section. Off my son and I went to the lake. He became frustrated with only snagging logs. Thankfully, a neighbor and his son invited us to join them. Their strategies were working. Before long, my son felt a tug. This was no log. What a thrill to watch him reel in that fish.

As we fish for kids, knowing how to catch their attention and reel them in is key. What influences kids? They are involved in sports . . . one for each season of the year. However, these games do not result from spontaneous play. Kids can enjoy a skateboard but will skillfully maneuver a skateboard even longer on an Xbox. Computers and burning a CD or DVD is no big deal to them. Music videos communicate fashion and much of this generation's culture. Kids text message and are influenced by the Internet, as well as hours of Disney, the Cartoon Network, Nickelodeon, and a zillion other television choices. In the midst of all of this technology, what can the church offer?

Relationships

Theologian Leonard Sweet shared with me that "Relationship issues stand at the heart of postmodern culture. The more digitally enhanced the culture becomes, the more flesh and blood human the enchantment. The more impersonal the transaction, the deeper the hunger is for relationship and community."

How can we help kids connect with friends in a church setting?

Children want to bring their friends along to share experiences. Their alternative to adults' "coffee and donut" time includes these hands-on activities offered as they arrive.

- **Giant** white board. A four-by-eight-foot sheet of shower board costs about $8 at most hardware stores. Glued to the classroom wall, it becomes a place for artistic expression that friends can share. Writing from dry erase markers can be removed with paper towels—a more thorough cleaning can be done with baby wipes.
- **Lego** blocks. Lego tables for elementary-age children can be constructed by attaching Lego base pieces to a tabletop. Even a used card table can fit this need and can become a popular place for children to create and talk. Parents of teenagers may donate kids' old Legos.
- **Silver Links** note cards. Some children enjoy artistic

activities. Once a month the choice is offered of making note cards. A volunteer reviews and delivers the cards to residents of senior citizen homes. The impact of this ministry can be far-reaching, as shared in a sermon at our church. It was recounted how a member of our church had arrived to visit her mother who had recently been moved to a senior citizen home. On the door of her mother's room, the woman found a card from one of the children from our church. With tears she expressed her sincere appreciation for the reminder that her mother had not been forgotten.

- **Small group** discussions. All three of the components that children need—relationships, experiences, and spiritual insight—can be facilitated during the small group time. Discussion means talking with kids, not at them. Ask open-ended questions that solicit feelings and thoughts, rather than yes-no answers. We get more information from children with a question that asks "Why?" or "How would you feel?" Even during the large group session, invite kids to "pair-share."

Experiences

Kids accumulate adventures and shared experiences—helping them to learn. While watching a skilled performer is an acceptable vicarious experience, children are not always satisfied with passive entertainment.

What kind of experiences make kids excited about coming back week after week? Kids will come back for the fun. We then can guide their attention toward biblical truths. Did you know that smiles positively impact the brain in children?

- **Games.** Activities that reinforce the lesson theme can help kids remember the key truth. They can quickly connect the fun with the lesson focus, but variety needs to be offered from week to week. *Making Fun Out of Nothing at All* by Anthony and Mike Burcher (Abingdon Press, 2004) is a great game idea book.
- **Memory** game. Predetermine an array of gadgets that reinforce your theme. Invite an even number of children to select from your supply. Each child will secretly hold an item behind his or her back. For example, if the theme is God's protection, then the gadgets could include two potholders, bottles of sunscreen, umbrellas, and tubes of toothpaste. A contestant will choose two participants in the lineup to show their hidden items. If they match, then play continues. If not, a second contestant will have a turn. Play continues until all items are matched. The connection to the lesson theme can and should be made.
- **Speed** Stacking. Almost ten thousand schools participate in the Speed Stacks sport program. Visit www.speedstacks.com for video examples of the play and information about the experience that continues to grow in popularity. Creative teachers may guide the children to discover an application with the teaching theme or simply add this to a slate of rotating activities.

- **The website** www.childrensministry.net lists a catalog of ideas, individuals, and ministry organizations focused on effective learning experiences for children.
- **Mission** projects. Making a difference through a meaningful experience is important to kids. Monetary giving is higher when a container is provided, such as the ark bank for the **Heifer Project.**

Heifer International seeks to end world hunger by providing livestock to poor families. The animals provide a source of milk, eggs, and wool and an offspring to give to another family in need. **Operation Christmas Child** is an inspiring mission project. Children gift wrap shoe boxes filled with donated school supplies. One church linked their Vacation Bible School story about Joseph with a **County Foster Care** organization. Donations included beach towels, swimsuits, goggles, and money for children in the foster care program to participate in summer sports. An art project included knotting fringe on fleece pillows and attaching a note of encouragement to a child in the foster care program. Each note was edited to make sure it was appropriate.

- **Relevant** music promotes movement and worship. Popular songs are those often used in adult contemporary worship. Children sing songs from the depth of their own need, such as "Making Him the Hero of My Life" and "I'm Trading my Sorrows." Look for affordable music at www.childrensministryjukebox.com. *Dance Praise* can turn a computer into an interactive movin' and groovin' experience. *Dance Praise* is a Christian alternative to the popular Dance Dance Revolution game. Visit the www.digitalpraise.com site to see why kids love this experience.

Spiritual Things

"Spiritual" does not necessarily mean "religious" for kids. Leonard Sweet's insight that spiritual experiences can become part of a collection and not necessarily a life-changing practice makes our role even more important.

How can we make our teaching relevant, so it is not lost in the clutter of culture?

Today's children can learn the truth of 2 Timothy 3:14-15,"But as for you, continue in what you have learned and have become convinced of, because you know those from whom you learned it, and how from infancy you have known the holy Scriptures, which are able to make you wise for salvation through faith in Christ Jesus" (NIV). Involve the parents. Even the toddlers and preschoolers tend to quickly respond to the class session when their parents talk with them about the weekly take-home paper.

- **Scripture** memorization. What we memorize as children can stay with us for a lifetime. Challenge elementary students to memorize key verses. Putting scripture verses to music is an effective memory technique. Some children respond positively to incentives. The incentive may simply be stamping a card stock bookmark after that week's verse is recited. One mother had a question because her family was planning a trip over the weekend. Her son was excited about learning the verses and winning prizes. She asked, "Is there any way he can recite the verse to someone before or after this weekend? He can memorize it by Wednesday night." Our rules must facilitate the ultimate goal . . . the thrill of learning God's Word.
- **Time** for renewal. Churches are offering camps on cheerleading, soccer, martial arts, and golf. Camps score high with kids, especially if the spiritual component is included. Camp registration fees may cover the cost of leasing a gymnasium. A lead coach guides the morning and afternoon sessions; the supporting coaches are volunteer parents and youth. Children improve their sport skills, which is a positive outcome. The critical result of

the week, though, is spiritual growth. A daily devotional and prayer focus is vital. One dad was pleased with what he heard about basketball camp, but the best report was seeing his son praying and reading his Bible.

- **Spiritual** benchmarks. A third-grade Bible presentation can provide lifelong memories. Congregation members may be reminded of their role in the spiritual development of the children. A year ago, when our third-grade Bible presentation was announced, a tenth grader asked the pastor if he could get a new Bible. He had been using the Bible given to him as a third grader so much that it was falling apart. How heartwarming to see him among those presented with a new Bible.

- **Bible** exploration. Offer the third graders an event to learn about the Bible. Tell the history—how our need for the Savior unfolds. Allow time for prayer. Adult table leaders may escort the children to a craft area to decorate a Bible jacket or a game, such as a friendly round of "Who Wants to be a Bible-aire?" Even the snack time can reinforce a Bible truth.

Can one person lead all of the Children's Ministry programs that are available?

Balance the amount of time that can be given by key leaders with the support of volunteers. Your church leaders must decide which vibrant, relevant programs you want to develop. People are excited to get involved in activities that are making a difference.

- **Family** Advent Night allows families to focus on the true meaning of the season while making a memory. During the first weekend of December, open the church building for a potluck or pizza dinner. Each family then makes an Advent craft. This event can easily link with a children's Christmas program, creating a night of preparation and anticipation. Our church provided supplies for three Chrismons, one for the family, one to hang on a church tree, and a third Chrismon was packaged with a flier highlighting service times to give to an unchurched family. This evangelism approach will be utilized again because of the positive response.

- **A Birthday** Party for Jesus can happen during Sunday school, on Saturday morning, or a weeknight. Children bring unwrapped toys for an organization, such as Toys for Tots, sponsored by the U.S. Marine Corps Reserve. Our church invites a young Marine in uniform to accept the toys at our party. Games and cupcakes are part of the party. The event ends with a presentation of the Christmas story by a puppet team or guest storyteller. A group of homeschooled children could make this their school play too.
- **Fall** Festival and "Trunk or Treat" are fun alternatives to Halloween. Adult Sunday school classes or small groups may take responsibility for organizing games inside the building or in the church parking lot. Complete the fun with candy and trinket prizes. *The Un-Halloween Book* (www.onewaystreet.org) is filled with creative activities for a successful event. Another good source of ideas is *Seasons of Faith* by Marcia Stoner (Abingdon Press, 2004).
- **Easter** preparation should include rich spiritual moments for the children, not just anticipating an Easter egg hunt. One meaningful experience is constructing Resurrection Eggs. The following items are needed for each child: one egg carton, twelve

ST-CUTTING

plastic eggs, a piece of palm branch, a drop of perfume, a cracker, one coin, a small paper cross, a thorn, a small nail, a piece of sponge, whole cloves or piece of cinnamon stick, a small rock, and a piece of white fabric. The children place each item in a plastic egg. One of the eggs will remain empty for the empty tomb. This tool can be used to tell the story of Jesus' resurrection. Involving the children in a **Palm Branch processional** provides another meaningful experience. Instead of purchasing real palms, the children may create a branch from construction paper.

When I asked Sara why she comes to church, it was her friend who answered first, "I come to be with her because she is my best friend." Sara then added to her friend's comment, "I come to see my friends and what we do is fun. I also like learning about God." Sara defined today's children and their three areas of need. Children today want relationships and experiences, and they are interested in spiritual things. We must focus on meeting those three needs.

Chapter Five

Programs That Move the Ministry Forward . . . More than Floating

Fishing vessels of all sizes and shapes are docked in marinas from one U.S. coast to another. Some of these boats are made for recreational use and others for commercial markets. Whether paddling on a lazy river, cruising along scenic waterways, or sailing on a pristine lake, the right boat makes a world of difference in fulfilling the desired results.

As with boats, a variety of approaches in Children's Ministry can be used to move our mission forward. Some programs are costly, but worth it. Some accommodate a limited number of children. There are programs designed to reach unchurched children. It is good to determine the desired outcomes when assessing programs; some may need time in dry dock for repairs. It could be time to implement new programs. In other words, do whatever it takes to provide memorable experiences so kids are learning and want to keep coming back for more.

Rethinking Traditional Programs

The vision of The Church of the Resurrection, "To transform lives, to transform our community and to renew the mainline church," is accomplished through worship, evangelism, service, discipleship, and fellowship. These five areas of ministry are incorporated into Children's Ministries, as well. The programs we offer include time for singing and prayer. Children have the opportunity to know Christ as their Savior and grow in their knowledge of the Bible. They are routinely provided occasions to put their faith into action through mission projects. Inviting and being with friends is vital to meeting their fellowship need. Whether you offer one program or many, the experiences children have at church should be among their most exciting experiences.

Sunday School

The Bible story was about the time Jesus prepared a meal on the beach for the disciples. It sounded like a barbeque to me, so I hung a volleyball net across the room and replaced the tables and chairs with beach towels. When Justin entered the room, he twisted his hips and with a thumbs-up announced, "It's a beach party!" Justin's response was worth the effort that went into creating the environment to hold his attention that Sunday morning.

Sunday school remains the primary Christian education vehicle in churches everywhere. With that fact in mind, we must keep the program vibrant. From the moment the classroom doors are opened, volunteers should be ready to make a positive connection with each child. Have supplies ready and a lesson plan listing effective methods for a relevant and fun hour. While Christian education is a serious topic, it cannot be boring. Every component of the experience should energize the hour.

Which curriculum is the best?
While most publishers do a good job of addressing the active-learning needs of today's child, all curriculums work best when the specific concerns for your congregation are considered. That means customizing the curriculum to fit your needs, your building, and your budget. Adapting does not mean lowering the standard of excellence.

Customizing the curriculum. One person or a small team of writers may select activities from the curriculum and enrichment materials. Include discussion questions in the lesson plan to help your leaders guide the conversation. List the supply needs on your customized lesson plan. Distribute the lesson plan to the volunteers so they can come prepared to engage each child. The rewriting process takes place weeks before the lesson is implemented. Published curriculum should be ordered as early as possible.

A Large Group/Small Group Format. This approach is used to facilitate quality story/music presentations, and it allows time for the leaders to connect with each child. The activities at the beginning of the session may link to the theme and should also meet the fellowship need for children. A large room is best for movement during the singing and drama time but is not required.

A Sample Small Group/Large Group Sunday Schedule:

8:50—9:05 **Small group** leaders welcome each child at classroom check-in. Offer floor/table games or lesson/craft activities for fellowship time. Then, clean up.

9:05—9:40 Gather into a **large group.** Leaders welcome the kids, pray, and lead

	from two to three songs with motions. Reinforce the memory verse with effective methods, connect the theme with a game, present a dramatized story and a life application.
9:40—10:05	Move to **small groups.** Guides will ask open-ended questions, present a responsive learning activity, and pray for joys and concerns. Listen and relate before preparing for dismissal.
10:05—10:15	Children may be involved in an activity as parents arrive.

The Large Group session includes music, the Bible story, and a life application. Invite volunteers who are comfortable with music and storytelling. Add motions to preselected songs to engage the children and reinforce the lesson theme. The *Every Move I Make* album (ZonderKidz, 2003) is an example of music that kids prefer. Storytellers who employ a variety of dramatic presentation methods can make the Bible come alive. Help kids connect the Bible story to their lives. *Movie Clips for Kids* (Group Publishing, 2001) lists ways to add a twist to the life application portion of the lesson.

Small Group. Small group leaders will get to know each child's name and build relationships as they guide the **activities, responses,** and **prayer time.** The goal of the interaction is to help the children capture the theme of the lesson and see how it applies to their lives. It is important for leaders to allow time for the kids to think and respond. This is not a traditional lecture time. The group may sit at a classroom table or on the floor in the corner of the classroom. Closing with a joys and concerns prayer time is vital.

> A volunteer prepared a color, cut, and paste activity as defined by the "customized" curriculum. The idea looked good on paper, but only one child actually chose the activity during the large group welcoming time. Other children were constructing a scene with Legos and completing jigsaw puzzles. It is wise to evaluate the plans and make changes, especially when we missed the mark.

Workshop Rotation Model. Traditional Sunday school may not always incorporate strategies to meet the children's different learning styles. The "one size fits all" method is the usual approach. In the Workshop Rotation Model, teachers present the same Bible story several times over a four- to six-week period using their own learning style and gifts. The children have a variety of experiences that reflect Howard Gardner's theory of multiple intelligences. A leader, or shepherd, escorts a group of children to the various workshops. These shepherds build caring relationships and meet the administrative needs, such as taking attendance and collecting the offering. Learn more about the Workshop Rotation Model at www.powerXpress.com.

Special Needs Ministry

There is no stipulation in God's Word that says only if they can walk, if they can talk, and if they understand like everyone else, then teach them. We are exhorted to let everyone come. This can only happen for some in our community if we create an inclusive barrier-free environment. Some children will get more from the teaching time if one-on-one assistance is arranged. In our Special Needs Ministry, an angel care provider may meet the parents and child. These volunteers patiently focus on the individual needs of the child and support the efforts of the classroom teacher. This ministry is often respite care for the parents. Whether your congregation is large or small, caring for the needs of all children can be shared among members of the congregation. You may want to invite a special education teacher to share effective strategies to help your volunteers.

Midweek programs

It makes sense to use successful methods in more than one area. That is why the Large Group/Small Group format may be incorporated into other programs. Families are busy, and offering programs at times other than the weekend can be a stretch. However, exciting options can capture the attention of children—and their parents will come along. So, getting the help you need may be easier than anticipated.

CLOSER LOOK

- **Flexible scheduling**. It may be too much to start a midweek program the same week as the new Sunday school year kicks off. Families get so many plates spinning that the midweek option becomes just that . . . an option. The calendar holds part of the solution. Use a semester approach. Start the midweek program a few weeks into September. End the first semester in early December. The second semester may begin in mid-January and last until the end of April. Parents appreciate this adaptation and kids are left wanting more. Instead of saying, "When is it going to end?" they say, "Is it over already?"
- **Short time frame.** Consider starting the program at 6:15 p.m. and dismissing at 7:30 p.m. This time frame works well. Families have time to eat a quick dinner, participate in the church program, and meet their school-night bedtime curfew.

- **Kindergarten to Fourth Grade Connection.** Children in kindergarten through fourth grade learn quite well in a mixed-age environment. A leader-to-child ratio of 1:5 accommodates positive interactions and makes a manageable size for younger and older children. Usually, a mom or dad of one or two of the children in the small group serves as the leader. Bandannas in different colors may help identify the groups and create a team feeling. Kids and leaders may tie the bandanna on their head, neck, arm, or an ankle. The Large Group session includes singing, announcements, and a skit. An effective skit adaptation is to read the script aloud while students mime the actions of the script. The kids move by groups to a Craft Station and Game Station or Surprise Station and Snack Station. Consider preregistration to help you plan. A registration fee may cover the cost of curriculum and supplies. Such fees often reinforce the value of the event and increase the commitment. Have fun naming the midweek program so the purpose is defined. One program is called the ZONE, which means:

  Z ealous for God
  O neness through relationships
  N urtured in truth
  E xpressing love for Christ

One mother reported that her son was so excited about ZONE that he wanted to skip soccer practice so he could be at the church. She stayed one night to watch the vibrant singing time and the kids moving to their stations. Then she observed the serious responses during the journal time. This mother joined other parents in proclaiming the benefits of midweek programming and signed on as a volunteer.

- **Upper Elementary.** By fifth grade a little different program is needed. Offering these kids a "youth group" approach can be a dynamic decision. Some churches put the fifth and sixth graders together. Older elementary students need a biblical perspective on the decisions they face. A strong leader should plan each week around relevant topics. Helpful resources include Gordon and Becki West's book *Dynamic Preteen Ministry: The Essential Guide to Build a No-Miss Ministry with Kids* (Group Publishing, 2000) and *Smart Choices for Preteen Kids* edited by Jim Hawley (Group Publishing, 1999). Periodically inviting guest speakers can enhance the program and support the themes. Guests might include an instrumentalist whose talent is being used in worship services. Or, a long distance runner might describe the steps needed to prepare for a race. It is easy to connect with the biblical theme of running the faith race. Serving food every week may be a stretch, but having pizza once a month is welcomed. Ask the children to contribute to the "pizza fund" and have them bring a package of snack food as well. Following the same time frame as the other midweek programs is wise.

➪ **Alpha Sprouts.** Look at effective adult programs for new ways to meet the needs of children. One church wanted to offer more than babysitting while the adults were involved in the ten-week exploration in Christianity called Alpha (www.alpha.org). Crossroads Christian Church in Corona, California, decided to adapt the Alpha course for their elementary-age children. Alpha Sprouts is offered at the same time as the parents' Alpha class. The kids meet from 6:30 to 8:30 p.m. The children start with a meal, just as the adults do. The children and an adult or youth table leader discuss the question for the session. Lives are being changed through this dynamic approach.

Vacation Bible School

Vacation Bible school has been around for a long time as a traditional summer program. Most publishers pack creative thematic activities into their VBS curriculum. Even so, a few changes may be necessary to fit the needs of your community. Even substituting the word "camp" for "school" is fun.

Assemble a leadership team. Each member of the team can share the responsibilities of the program. Some churches create their own thematic approach. Our church used a "Fifties" theme for "Peter and the Rock 'n' Roll Bible Show" and a country theme with "Joseph and the Technicolor Overalls." A talented storyteller or a small troupe of actors can present the Bible story with dramatic flair. Link the music with meaningful motions. Secure a quality CD player for the week to enhance the background music. Charging a registration fee may allow you to provide each child with a T-shirt or economical backpack imprinted with the name of your church and the program theme. Your Children's Ministry will be advertised each time a child wears the item.

- **Churches** in smaller communities have joined forces for a dynamic summer program. A leader from each participating church takes responsibility for one component of the week. If none of the church buildings in your community are large enough to host the children, then a city park and pavilion may be an ideal setting. Consider offering the program in the evening so working parents can participate as volunteers.
- **A Backyard** Club format is effective in some communities. Transportation challenges are eliminated and children whose parents do not value attendance at a church event may allow them to visit a

neighbor's club. Screening volunteers and adequately staffing each club is required to reduce child safety risks. Hosting a final club at the church building is one way to introduce nonreligious families to the church. A pizza dinner or dessert with highlights of the games, stories, and songs can be a fun, nonthreatening family event.

A few years ago I made the decision to include a pet show in our study about Noah. At the beginning of the day, the children could bring their pets. Parents came along to take the pets home immediately following the Show and Tell. A mother introduced their pet bird to me. She let me know that their bird had heart trouble. Well, needless to say the environment was anything but calm. Dogs were barking, cats meowing, and fish were flopping. The bird survived and the kids loved the plan, but it was nerve-racking for the leaders. Smile if you must, but I'm not sure I would repeat that idea.

Evaluate

It does not take long to get comfortable with doing things the same way year after year. However, the same routine can get old. In 1986, a friend of mine introduced Market Place 29 A.D. to her congregation as an alternative approach to traditional Vacation Bible School. With some adaptations, the curriculum was used two other summers. After retiring from her job as director of Children's Ministries, my friend's innovative idea was used at the church for the next twelve years. Innovations cease to be innovations with this kind of repetition.

I am convinced that relevant churches make annual modifications. Evaluation is necessary for effective Children's Ministry.

To determine if your goals are being met, ask if the program is:
Biblically sound?
Creatively inviting?
Facilitating a response?
Paced to not drag?
Incorporating relevant popular music?
Fulfilling for the volunteers?
Involving an appropriate ratio of volunteers?
Ending with kids talking about the fun and what they learned?

Although Will has always attended a church, his mother had never heard him express excitement about his involvement until now. A job change had created the situation that brought Will's family to their new church. Will, a shy fifth grader, told his mother everything about that first Sunday, "It was great! We are never going to miss! We learned about 2 Kings 4, and we played this game, and I met this boy, and . . ."

After hearing this report, I visited with Will to learn more about why he was excited and what he liked. "The game time at the beginning was good. I like Four Square and I met some kids. I like the songs. The small group was good." When I asked what was different from his previous experiences at church, Will just remembered waiting in the classroom until the teacher started telling the story. He thought that was boring. It was the experience, the relationship, and the spiritual focus that captured Will. That is what Children's Ministry must offer every week. Sitting in a classroom waiting for the stuff to begin will not create the kind of excitement that says, "We are never going to miss!"

CHAPTER SIX

Staying the Course

One Sunday morning I tried to soothe the troubled feelings of a two-and-one-half year old. Steven was not happy. He let everyone in the classroom and everyone down the hall know how miserable he was. The old finger play, *"Here is the church. Here is the steeple. Open the door. See all the people."* was used to calm him. My toddler friend had his own version. He put his little hands over mine and cried, "Here are da people. Close da door and wet's go home."

We smile, but there may be times when we want to "close da door." Early in my first assignment as a director of Children's Ministries, I felt overwhelmed. This job opportunity had unfolded in only three weeks, leaving little time to ponder the impact of moving six hundred miles. I had not been looking for a change in careers, but God had drawn a map for an exciting adventure. My experience as an educator and my involvement as a church volunteer gave me confidence. I sensed a calling to this first assignment. It did not take long to discover that church work is not all it appears to be—it is far more. Sadly, the first response of many overwhelmed leaders in Children's Ministry is permanently closing the door—quitting. Instead of quitting, I suggest we stop.

Yes, stop doing the things that drain and distract us. This may require a change of course to move toward strategies that help us focus on the reasons we accepted a role in Children's Ministries—focus on the mission of what God wants to accomplish.

Climb Aboard

Step 1: Pace with a Mentor

Soon after starting my first job on staff, I met the representative from the curriculum publisher that our church used. He introduced me to an experienced director of Children's Ministries from a neighboring church. Her denomination was different than mine, but that did not matter. This godly woman knew things about being a director that I did not know, and she became a valued mentor. At lunch one day she said, "Give the job at least two years. You will want to quit numerous times, but don't. Something wonderful will happen by the end of those two years." She was right! I learned a lot about working with volunteers and developing leaders. I also came to understand the value of connecting with peers who share my passion. Linking with those who have rich insight into ministry and developing friendships with others who share this noble calling have sustained me.

- **Link** with a Christian Education group. Connect with leaders through your denomination or a regional publishing representative. Some reps actively facilitate collegial meetings. Do not limit yourself only to your denomination or your curriculum publisher. Step outside the box.
- **Attend** a conference. There is something about getting away to enhance your skills and get spiritually renewed. Conferences also become great places for professional connections. Conferences, such as

the Leadership Institute (www.cor.org) and Children's Pastors' Conference (www.incm.org), can be a source of lifelines and ideas.

- **Develop** trusted friendships. Ministry is not for the Lone Ranger. Connect with someone from another church who shares the same job description. My best friends share my passion for Children's Ministries. We brainstorm ideas, listen to each other's challenges, pray together, and even give caring correction. I do not know what I would do without these friends who really understand.

Step 2: Establish Trust

While hosting a meeting of key Children's Ministry leaders, I made arrangements for us to visit a couple of ministries in Detroit. After being inspired at the Community Development Center in southwest Detroit, we drove to a historic church near the New Center area where I had been helping. As we entered the massive stone sanctuary, one of the men commented, "You can feel the tradition in this place. How have you been able to bring change to Children's Ministry?"

The answer to that question rests in trust. Our role in Children's Ministry was offered because of our skill and passion and a response to the Holy Spirit's whisper. Responsibility for the ministry rests on our shoulders, but how we conduct ourselves and lead the ministry can impact our relationship with the pastor.

- **How** can a positive working relationship be established? How do I get the pastor to trust me with the new ideas I want to implement?

  Trust does not happen overnight. It is established by the "precept upon precept" principle. A misstep may mean we go back to the starting line in the trust race. Think about the people you trust. They exude integrity, responsibility, and respect.

- **Work** with integrity. Integrity is not only about being a person of our word and not stealing paper clips. Integrity also includes an honest use of our attention and our time. Focus on church work while on the church's "time clock." Make your commitment to the vision of the church evident. Good or bad, we are never really off the clock. People in the congregation look to us with certain expectations. Integrity is important in the office, in a store, on the road, at our kids' school, in a restaurant . . . wherever we are, integrity counts.
- **Manage** responsibly. Take on projects that count. There are plenty of distractions that are noble, but they may not impact the vision. Learn to use computer software to help improve your ability to manage. Take fiscal responsibility. We are handling "holy" money. Learn about budgets and what the bookkeeper needs.

When we moved into our new building, we were thrilled with the space that was designated for storage. Unfortunately, our supplies did not get organized before three hundred notebooks were purchased. We already had three hundred notebooks, but they were in an unlabeled box. Yes, we eventually used them, but the purchase at that time was unnecessary. Lack of organization of the supplies had impacted my fiscal responsibility.

- **Respect** the pastor's need for information. Pastors welcome innovations. However, pastors do not like surprises. Years ago, the pastor I worked with telephoned me on a Saturday afternoon. A dad had called the parsonage asking if the second graders should be picked up at the church. I had made an assumption that the pastor had more important things to consider than the second grade class party and had not listed the event during our staff meeting reports. It was my responsibility to keep the pastor informed—the pastor will determine the value of the information. I learned a lesson on trust that day.

Step 3: Delegate Authority

- **What** can I do to make myself more efficient? I feel overwhelmed.

  Delegate authority. One Sunday morning I used a puppet in a children's sermon. This tried and true tool was a hit for that congregation. A group of women in the church offered to purchase the supplies if I would start a puppet team. Having led a team in the past, I knew what to do. Time, not skill, was the issue. I could not take on another responsibility. Teresa was a new member of the church. She had been a dance major in college and since puppet teams use the same methods as synchronized dance, Teresa's abilities would fit like a hand in a glove. She welcomed the invitation to lead the team. I provided her initial training and ordered an instructional video from www.onewaystreet.com. This delegation was a win-win for Teresa and the ministry.

  Learn to say "NO" to the add-ons. Admitting that you do not have time for another task is not a bad thing. If you struggle saying no, delay the need to respond. Give yourself time to consider by saying, "Let me think about it and get back to you," or compromise with, "I can't do that, but I will do this."

Step 4: Collaborate Instead of Compete

"If our department is not number one on the pastor's priority list, then we are nothing." This crippling expectation exists among staff members in many congregations. Competition with other ministry areas is not healthy, even when it appears we are at the bottom. Statistician George Barna's survey of pastors places Children's Ministry as number ten on the pastors' ranking of importance. (See page 9.) Pastors in the Kansas East Conference of The United Methodist Church placed children and youth as number four out of the five most important characteristics of a vital congregation. Yes, Children's Ministry is essential, and I am passionate about the work we do. However, these surveys tell us that a pastor has many issues to address. There are numerous vital characteristics in a congregation, and we are one part of the big picture. A positive perspective might be that we are handling things so well that we do not require the pastor's continual intervention.

When I asked pastors to provide their expectations for Children's Ministries, the following responses were given:

- The adults who work with children will communicate love and acceptance.
- Children's Ministry will reflect the vision of the church.
- The children will learn that God loves them and sent Jesus as their Savior.
- The children will grow to become devoted disciples in mission to the world.
- The children will be safe from predators when they are in our care.
- Parents will learn how to be a positive spiritual influence.

These responses provide evidence that pastors have a handle on what an effective Children's Ministry should provide. Let's rejoice!

➪ **Will** you join me in applying the following guidelines?

- No whining "poor me" attitude allowed.
- No complaining background noise. Rather than moan about our lack, we will focus on the role we play in the overall growth of our church.
- Present solutions, not problems. Collaboration will help us accomplish the vision of the church. Show that the needs of the organization are a priority for you whether or not they are part of your job description.

"Steer the ship of my life, good Lord, to your quiet harbor, where I can be safe from the storms of sin and conflict. Show me the course I should take. Renew in me the gift of discernment, so that I can always see the right direction in which I should go. And give me the strength and the courage to choose the right course, even when the sea is rough and the waves are high, knowing that through enduring hardship and danger in your name we shall find comfort and peace."

—Basil of Caesarea c. 330-379

Step 5: Make Healthy Choices

Do not forget that your body is the temple of the Holy Spirit (I Corinthians 6:19). The mindset that equates spirituality with doing more and more can leave us physically drained, spiritually dry, and emotionally isolated. Neglecting your health is dangerous. We are inundated with information on personal health. However, knowing and doing are two different things.

Dr. Pam Harris, a physician in the Kansas City area, offers these approaches to stay balanced in body, mind, and spirit:

- Have a checkup before any major changes in diet or exercise.
- Follow through with recommended screening examinations.

- Exercise without diet and diet without exercise tend to fail as weight control strategies.
- Sleep eight hours a night.
- Watch what you feed your brain. Garbage in . . . garbage out. (See Philippians 4:8.)

Step 6: Find Joy in Your Work

What can I do to feel appreciated and not focus on negative experiences?

The pastor of a church in Michigan says qualities he seeks in a director of Children's Ministries include hardworking and winsome with a noncomplaining spirit.Try these simple but helpful strategies to discover joy:

Start a "goodie file." Tuck away thank you notes. Periodically read a few of them to remind yourself of how your work impacts others.

Expect change. Usually the only person who likes change is a wet baby. Anticipate that few things in life are constant. One coping method is to do routine tasks in new ways. Drive to work on a different route. Discovering better ways to do everyday activities can be fun.

Seek sources of strength and joy:

- Read biographies of faith. Surround yourself with courageous people.
- Hang out with people who smile. Visit www.reverendfun.com.
- Affirm others. Appreciation is contagious.
- Make a play date with friends. My team sets aside a few hours every other month for a BRIDGE day. We **B**uild **R**elationships **I**n **D**efined **G**roup **E**vents. Activities we have participated in have included taking a prayer walk through a flower garden, preparing a meal under the

guidance of a chef, visiting an interior design studio, and eating breakfast at a favorite restaurant.

Keep jumping in!

I hope my little song brings a smile to your face and reminds you of the reason we do what we do. Please hum to the tune of "Sixteen Tons."

I woke one mornin' heard the church bells ring,
Turned on the PowerPoint® and started to sing,
I'm on staff at the church, just the kids and me,
I got sixteen jobs, plus my own family.

Sixteen jobs and what do you get?
Another day older, but I love it, you bet,
Saint Peter, don't you call me 'cause I can't go,
Have a meeting at one and Kids' Choir at four.

Need to talk with the head of the nursery,
A mother went wild, caused some misery,
Macaroni and salad for dinner tonight,
Throw a load in the wash. Things will be all right!

I try so hard and what do I get?
Hearing people's troubles 'til I might regret,
I took this position when I saw the need,
The Lord will give me what I need to succeed.

The Lord will give me a new VBS head,
Now that Mrs. Jones said the program is dead,
Got to get to the mall cause my kids need clothes,
The pastor just called, there's no time to doze.

Be a children's leader and what do you get?
A host of friends and the fullest life yet,
Saint Peter, don't you call me, 'cause I can't go,
Want to help more kids come to know the Lord.

LINCOLN CHRISTIAN COLLEGE AND SEMINARY
115980

268.04
C739

At a recent family picnic, my three nephews entertained themselves with a cannonball contest into the swimming pool. The boys cried, "Watch me!" They wanted applause after each jump. As Children's Ministry directors, we may not shout out as loudly as my nephews did, but the desire for affirmation is still there. Jesus warned us, "Be careful not to do your acts of righteousness before men, to be seen by them" (Matthew 6:1 NIV). Affirmation is not bad, but focusing on the Kingdom reasons to serve brings lasting fulfillment. Doing a job that pleases God will result in inner joy that splashes out like water from a fountain.

Thank you for jumping in. Clap, clap, clap!

3 4711 00187 4827